TRAINING & ACTIVATION MANUAL

SPIRITUAL GIFTS

Course 1: Soaking Prayer, Speaking in Tongues & 30+ Types of Prayer

Servant Robin

TRAINING & ACTIVATION MANUAL; Course 1: 25 TYPES OF PRAYER; TONGUES & INTERPRETATION OF TONGUES

Copyright © 2012 Robin Jegede-Brimson
No part of this book may be reproduced or transmitted in any form or by any means, electronic, mechanical, photocopying and recording or by any information storage and retrieval system without written permission from the author.

All scripture quotations, unless otherwise indicated, are taken from the Holy Bible, New International Version®, NIV®. Copyright ©1973, 1978, 1984, 2011 by Biblica, Inc.™ Used by permission of Zondervan. All rights reserved worldwide. www.zondervan.com. The "NIV" and "New International Version" are trademarks registered in the United States Patent and Trademark Office by Biblica, Inc.™

"Scripture quotations taken from the Amplified® Bible, Copyright © 1954, 1958, 1962, 1964, 1965, 1987 by The Lockman Foundation. Used by permission." (www.Lockman.org)

3rd edition

Published by

SERVANT BOOKS www.servantbooks.co.uk

Distributed by

Robin Jegede-Brimson

Servant Ministries

7, Belton Close, Whitstable, Kent

CT5 4LG, UK

+44(0) 787 202 4364

GodsOyster@aol.com

AFRICA

Henry Hamilton

Servant Ministries Nigeria

U.I.P.O. Box 22974, Ibadan, Nigeria.

+234(0) 80 3368 1552.

hamiltonh78@hotmail.com

Cover design by

BARLT GRAPHICS PRINTS, NIG.

+234(0) 70 3822 8234

topekanbi@yahoo.com

*To my brother Paul and his wife Monica:
The way you love and the way you pray will always
inspire me.*

TYPES OF PRAYER

1. Priestly Prayer
2. Soaking Prayer
3. Intercessory Prayer
4. Prayer in the Spirit
5. Speaking in Tongues
6. Warfare Prayer; 'clearing the heavens'
7. Prayer of Thanksgiving
8. Prayer of Praise
9. Clapping Hands and Stamping Feet
10. Prayer of Worship
11. Soaking Worship
12. Prayer of Singing in The Spirit
13. The prayer for an Open Heaven towards GOD
14. Personal & Corporate Repentance,
15. Identificational Repentance - Preparing the Ground for Revival Rain
16. Petition
17. Supplication
18. Weeping
19. Prayer of Committal
20. Prayers of Dedication & Sanctification
21. Prayer of Submission to GOD
22. Prayers of Enquiry
23. Prayer of Agreement, Unity,
24. Binding & Loosing
25. Decrees & Proclamations
26. The Prayer of Faith
27. Prayer of rebuke, command
28. Prayer of Travail, Birthing & Groaning
29. Prayers for Healing
30. The Prayer of Deliverance
31. Pauline Prayers

CONTENTS

LESSON 1

INTRODUCTION

1Corinthians 14:15; 1Timothy 2:1; Ps 51; Matthew 9:6; Daniel 9; Nehemiah 1:5-7; Joshua 6:17; Acts 16:25; 1Samuel 4:4;

In this training manual we will look at 30+ different types of prayer and their different applications as we learn to grow in our relationship with GOD through The HOLY SPIRIT. Our dependence on The SPIRIT grows as we pray both with our natural minds (*'in understanding)* as well as in a more supernatural way through tongues (*'in the spirit'*). We'll grasp the relevance of times of devotion as spiritual "re-fuelling stations" as we journey through life. In a course after this first one we'll also look at the role of prophecy as well as other revelatory graces and how they impact both our prayer life and walk with GOD. At each section along the way we'll look at the gifts of The SPIRIT and see the invaluable part they play in our being able to keep the commandments of GOD; HIS commandments to pray effectively, communing with HIM & representing HIM effectively as we extend HIS Kingdom on Earth. After grasping and growing in prayer we'll move on in later courses to looking at the POWER or 'APOSTLIC' gifts as means through which GOD's purposes for HIS bride are fulfilled

Three questions . .

1. WHY STUDY PRAYER?

There are various types and shades of prayer as alluded to by the apostle Paul *"I exhort therefore that supplications, prayers, intercessions "* It becomes obvious as we grow in our relationship with The LORD that different situations require different types of prayer. e.g. In repentance from sin, we are to be meek, gentle and contemplative. At other times we are to be authoritative as in praying for healing or deliverance. We also find that there are times to weep as in Daniel's & Nehemiah's prayers for forgiveness for the sins of their people. Contrast this as when there are prayer times that require shouting as when surrounding the city of Jericho, or loud praise in the middle of the night while in prison. Discernment is needed as to what is required on each occasion e.g. shouting when there is need for another type of prayer proved disastrous.

Learning about different types of prayer does two things; firstly as we learn we practice each form of prayer in actual real prayer, so we pray. Secondly learning unlocks more of the potential for The HOLY SPIRIT to guide us in various forms of prayer. It is more difficult to yield to The HOLY SPIRIT and pray a certain way if a channel has not first been opened up in our thought patterns and understanding of scriptures to encompass those prayers.

Prayer is more than just asking our heavenly FATHER for our daily bread. There are laws that govern our relationship with HIM; Things that HE expects us to know and walk in which come from an understanding of HIS word. There are forces of evil that we as HIS representatives are required to deal with. A study of prayer makes us more useful and effective in The MASTER's Hands.

Joel 2:28; Numbers 11:29; 1Corinthians 14:1; 1Corinthians 14:31; John14:12; 1Corinthians 12:7;John 14:12

____

____

2. WHY STUDY PROPHECY?

At the birth of the church on the day of Pentecost, Peter stood up and preached from a passage of scripture that promises that all sons and daughters will one day prophesy. Moses, the deliverer of the children of Israel desired that all would prophesy. Paul the apostle also asked all who were in the church at Corinth to earnestly desire to prophesy, saying that they all could prophesy!

____

____

____

____

3. "GREATER THINGS " – SHOULD I BE INTERESTED?

Do we really believe JESUS' words, *'Truly I say to you they who believe in me shall do the works that I do, he will do even greater things than these because I go to The FATHER'*. It is JESUS's joy, desire and expectation that HIS ceiling become our floor. ***There are no miracles reserved for only the Bible. None.***

The gifts have been released on the Earth for everyone's benefit. GOD gives them to us through the work of The HOLY SPIRIT. If something is on offer by GOD Himself, it would be extremely presumptuous to say, 'No thanks, not for me mate'. Let's learn all we can, let's get all that's on offer. It will cost too much to let these gifts pass us by.

____

____

____

Questions

1. What should be my response to these things?

2. Does it matter how I respond?

3. Who is there to help me on my journey of discovery?

14

LESSON 2

PRAYER, THE SPIRIT, THE WORD & FASTING

Ephesians 4:30; James 1:19; 1Thessalonians 5:19

A definition

Prayer can be defined as interacting with the tangible, though physically imperceptible spiritual realm in order to impact the lesser, highly transient natural realm.

PRAYER & THE HOLY SPIRIT

Our ability to operate in the spiritual realm is very limited without the help of The HOLY SPIRIT who is our guide and helper. Effective prayer therefore comes out of our response to the promptings & leadings of The SPIRIT. As we interact with HIM more and more, our senses become accustomed to HIS touch, HIS leading & HIS Voice. As we grow we learn to yield to what HE says even when on occasion this conflicts with what people or circumstances seem to be saying.

Our overall effectiveness in prayer is hinged on

1. Our closeness, sensitivity, consecration and obedience to The HOLY SPIRIT
2. The level of faith our walk with GOD has exposed us to

TIPS TO GROWTH IN INTIMACY

❖ Treasure HIM, treasure HIS voice.

❖ Go on trysts (Old English for a date) with HIM.

❖ Don't grieve HIM.

❖ Be quick to repent.

❖ Don't quench the inner voice.

❖ Allow HIM flow through you.

What other <u>personal</u> tips has He given you to walk closer to Him?

____

____

PRAYER & THE WORD OF GOD

2Timothy 3:16; Psalm 1:1-3; 119:9,11; Luke 4:4; Joshua 1:6; Romans 4:16-21; 10:17; Jeremiah 15:16; Job 23:12

It is not possible to pray effectively without even a rudimentary grasp of what the Bible says. The more we know the Bible the more effective we can be in our prayers.

Through the Bible we gain
   a.   Understanding
   b.   Faith
   c.   Spiritual sustenance.

When we lead people in prayer this is one of the reasons why it is great to quote from The Word as it releases divine energy into peoples spirits before they engage in prayer or warfare.

The Word of GOD is to our hearts like food is to our body.
What's your daily intake? Would you consider yourself healthy as a result?

____

____

PRAYER & FASTING

Isaiah 58; 1Corinthians 9:24-27; Daniel9:3

Flow along with The HOLY SPIRIT, yield to HIM as HE prompts you to. HIS release of grace is the signal to fast. Sometimes this comes as an invitation, an inner feeling. Don't ignore it, when you say yes, grace will flow. Don't delay it; grace is something you grab on to while it's there! ☺

"Fasting releases new levels of the anointing into your life and ministry. it is a discipline that tests, trains and equips us to walk in power and authority, strengthening and transforming our inner self to carry greater levels of His glory"

"Certain victories will not be achieved in our lives or in the lives of others unless we combine prayer with fasting" (Pages 105 & 107 'The hidden power of Prayer and Fasting by Mahesh Chavda)

- ❖ **Total fasts** with no water or food. Never for more than 3 days to avoid injury to your health eg Ezra 8:21, 10:6; Esther 4:16

- ❖ **Normal fasts** like the one JESUS did where you drink water but don't eat.

- ❖ **Partial fasts** aka Daniel fasts where you abstain from certain foods or restrict yourself to just juices or salad. Daniel 10:2-3. Also apparently John the Baptist lived on a partial fast of only locusts and honey. Hence his power in preaching? Matthew 3:4.

- ❖ **Chain fasts**; with many people each taking a day or time slot

- ❖ Fast until 12noon, 6pm (you ask HIM when HE'd like you to break)

- ❖ 24 hour fasts; from one evening to the next. Can be very advantageous as you sleep fasting and this churns up your spiritual energy

- ❖ **3, 5, 7, 10, 21 or 40-day fasts.** For long fasts sometimes you may have a liberty to sustain yourself after several days with a glass of very diluted juice or a mug of water with some seasoning to replace body salts.

PRESS IN!

Pray along with the confessions from Isaiah 58. There are at least 12 blessings available there.

Honour HIS grace on your life, pray well and break well.

If you mess up in the fast, repent, draw fresh grace and press on! DON'T BE DISCOURAGED – pick up where you left off and allow yourself the luxury of a small sweet drink or so rather than abandon the whole thing.

TIP: There are three ways of being graced to consecrate a fast -

    A. As a weekly or regular discipline

    B. As you are prompted to by The HOLY SPIRIT

    C. In obedience to those in leadership over you as they call for a corporate fast

LESSON 3

DEVOTIONAL TIMES, PRIESTLY & INTERCESSORY PRAYER

YOUR PERSONAL DEVOTIONAL TIME

Scripture: *Psalms 65:4*

This is your prime relational time with The LORD. It should be at least once in a day, with imagination it could be several stopping times, places or "station" when you just shoot up a heart felt prayer to say, "THANK YOU LORD, I appreciate You!" and blow HIM a kiss! These times could be when you wake up, last thing at night, before meals, etc. The more meeting places you have the merrier! Each time is an opportunity for heavenly interaction and a download of grace, wisdom, refreshing, power . . .whatever you need! I learnt a very refreshing devotional habit (similar to an altar as we'll read later) as I noticed a habit of my sister in law, Monica. First thing she does when she's been out is she kneels by her bedside (or wherever) and says a quick "Thank You JESUS" prayer – try it - it's great. We can also view these devotional times as personal trysting places – where lovers meet! Allow HIM to draw you!

It is said of John Wesley's mother that when she could not find a place of quiet to get alone with GOD, she would simply cover her head with a shawl.

Consistent and thorough personal devotions are an essential prerequisite for growth and success in our purpose on Earth. View these times as when you receive fresh instructions from your headquarters in heaven.

____

____

FAMILY DEVOTIONAL TIME

Scripture: *Acts 10:24; Proverbs 22:6;*

Family meeting times and devotional habits. This includes fun times exploring the Bible and talking about life with our kids.

Note that the process of training entails: -

1. Teaching it
2. Demonstrating it
3. Ensuring that it is carried out

____

____

COMMUNITY DEVOTIONAL TIMES & AND NATIONAL REPENTANCE

2Chronicles chapter 7 & chapter 15; 1Kings chapter 18;

When as a nation and people we remember GOD's goodness to us and ask for HIS blessing or healing for our land. An example is when Winston Churchill asked the nation to pray every day at 12noon for protection from Nazi Germany. Recently we have seen over a million meet in prayer and fasting in Haiti.

Elijah needed to rebuild the altar before asking for the fire to fall.

____

____

BIBLICAL ALTARS

Joel 2; 2Chronicles 7:14; Genesis 26:19-25; 28:10-22;

There are similarities between our devotional times and altars in the Bible. In looking at what altars are and the spiritual principles behind them we can gain insight into the importance of our devotional times

- Altars can be defined as places of interaction between the physical and spiritual realms (Judges 13:8-22; John 1:51)

- Altars are erected by sacrifice; this could be blood, material wealth, convenience, power, prestige, position, etc - anything of value to the worshipper (Hebrew 13:15)

- Altars function as invitations to the spirit world (depending on to whom the sacrifices were either purposely or inadvertently made). They act as geographical entry points for spirits to invade and occupy territories on the Earth. (both good and evil)

- Altars are places of safety and refuge in times of danger (Genesis 34:30 – 35:5)

- Altars function as channels for the transfer of information (revelation), power & authority from the spiritual world to the natural world.

- The term altars can be used to refer to the times and places where GOD's people meet with HIM. These could be on a personal, family, church or office basis. Where I grew up in Nigeria, it is the norm in literally hundred's of thousands of businesses to set aside time at the start of each day for the workers to meet to pray and worship together!

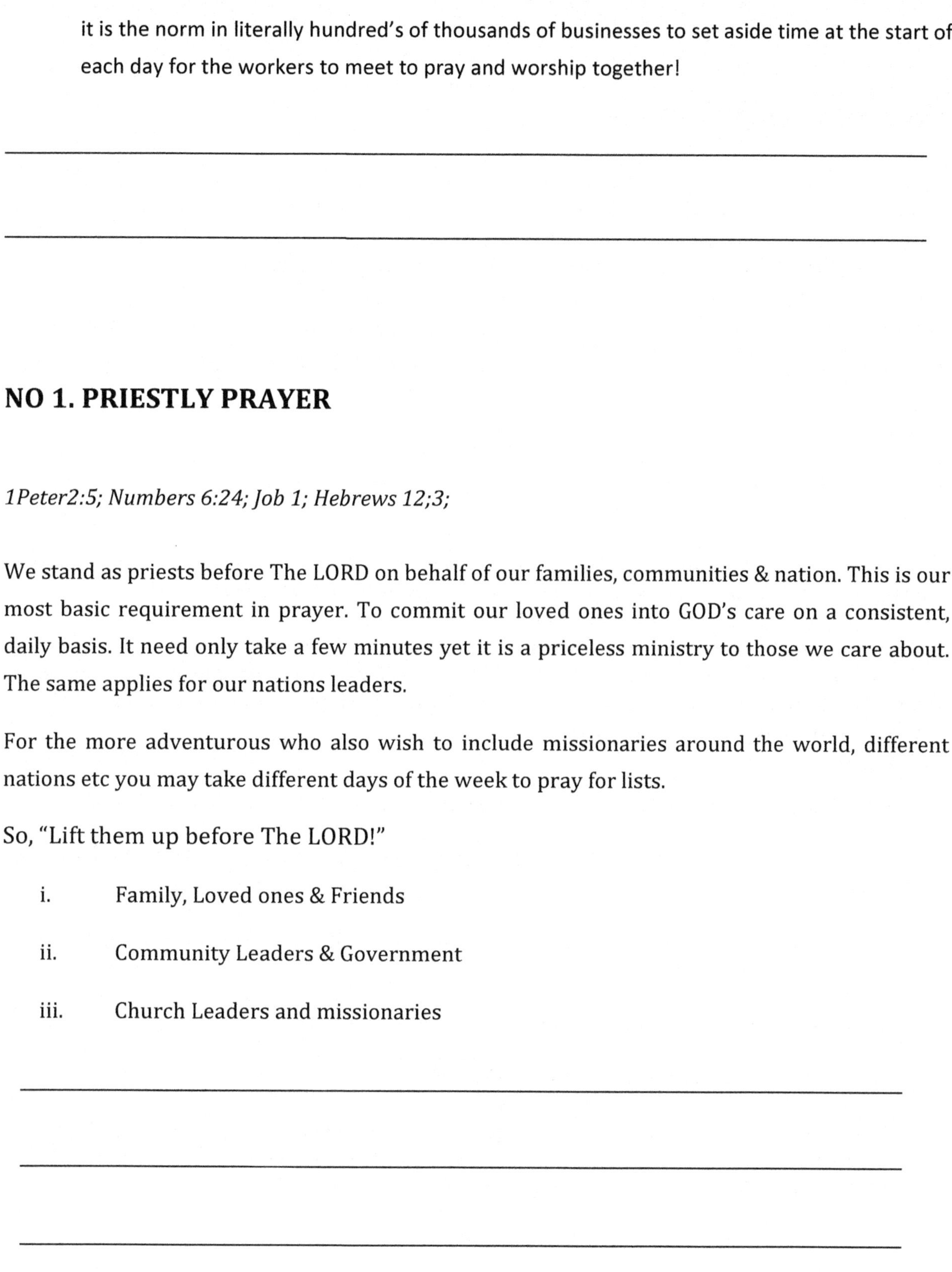

25

NO 1. PRIESTLY PRAYER

1Peter2:5; Numbers 6:24; Job 1; Hebrews 12;3;

We stand as priests before The LORD on behalf of our families, communities & nation. This is our most basic requirement in prayer. To commit our loved ones into GOD's care on a consistent, daily basis. It need only take a few minutes yet it is a priceless ministry to those we care about. The same applies for our nations leaders.

For the more adventurous who also wish to include missionaries around the world, different nations etc you may take different days of the week to pray for lists.

So, "Lift them up before The LORD!"

    i.   Family, Loved ones & Friends

    ii.   Community Leaders & Government

    iii.   Church Leaders and missionaries

NO 2. SOAKING PRAYER

There is great emphasis in recent times on this form of prayer as it leads to a realisation of our identity as special and unique members of Christ's Body. In the charismatic movement praying in tongues was the primary way to prepare for outreach, while obviously this is still very valid; it is being overtaken in emphasis with soaking prayer. So we'll spend quite a bit of time here.

Just being with Him; drawn into His atmosphere of love and peace and joy. Saturated in the warmth that exudes from Him. Soaking prayer also goes by the names, resting or waiting or tarrying in His Presence

How does this come about? Basically in the light of the truth that we become like the people we hang out with!

2 Cor. 3:18 "But we all, with unveiled face, beholding as in a mirror the glory of the Lord, are being transformed into the same image from glory to glory, just as by the Spirit of the Lord."

Song of Solomon 2: 3-5 "Like an apple tree among the trees of the woods, so is my beloved among the sons. I sat down in his shade with great delight, and his fruit was sweet to my taste. He brought me to the banqueting house, and his banner over me was love. Sustain me with cakes of raisins, refresh me with apples, for I am lovesick."

As we spend time with Him waiting in quiet in His Presence several things occur in our hearts:-

1. Healing comes to our souls. We become saturated with His love and Presence and inner healing flows

2. We learn to quiet the noise of our minds and receive His Peace without which direction is difficult to grasp (Isaiah 32:17)

3. Direction comes as He shows us the way to go (Psalm 16:11)

4. Identity is released as we rest before our FATHER.

5. Revelation is released as get to know more who He is and who we are. The Lord delights in revealing the secret counsel of His heart; dealing with issues that need to be addressed and bringing wisdom to our situation and needs. (Psalm 25:12-14)

6. Spiritual empowerment and fresh grace comes.

7. This also can lead to words of knowledge, and other revelatory gifts coming into operation.

Psalm 37:7 "Rest in the Lord, and wait patiently for Him."

When we soak in God's presence, we are in a place of rest where we wait upon Him. We become saturated With God. Soaking involves becoming saturated with God so that we take on God's flavour or nature. This is a logical step beyond taste and see that the LORD is good (Psalm 34:8)

When we soak in God's presence, we begin to behold Him. As we do, we become like Him. Soaking in God's presence enables us to behold the Lord. We cannot do this and remain the same. We are changed from glory to glory and transformed to be more like Him.

Is. 40: 31 "But those who wait on the Lord shall renew their strength; they shall mount up with wings like eagles, they shall run and not be weary, they shall walk and not faint."

This familiar verse reveals that something happens when we wait on God. Who He is, starts to get on us and in us. This divine exchange of His strength for our weakness and His ability instead of our frailty and inadequacy, happens because we spend time waiting on Him.

This article by Pam Watson, Secret Place Ministries is very informative. (Used by permission)

Soaking in God's presence is like coming and sitting in His shade and being fed with the fruit of His presence. Like the bride in the Song of Solomon, we can do this with great delight. This passage also speaks of the progression that usually follows where He brings us to the banqueting house or house of wine. This is something that only the Lord can do, but it starts with us coming and sitting in His presence. As we do so, so we are taken into deeper realms of experiencing His love for us, which is likened to being in a house of wine. This not only increases our love for the Lord, but can result in outward manifestations in those who have drunk the wine of His presence. It is not unusual for people to laugh, shake or cry and sometimes this experience is referred to as 'drinking'

Ps.46: 10 "Be still and know that I am God"

Again this exhortation tells us that when we are still or soaking in God's presence there will come a knowing or experiencing of God. There is a weight or glory to His presence that we can experience as we are still before Him. It is hard at times to come to this place though because our flesh is very active and often takes a while to settle. What we do with our bodies however is a powerful declaration in the realm of the spirit. When we lie down in God's presence it is a statement of surrender and a posture of rest that the Lord will honour.

It helps to play worship music while we are soaking. Music sets the atmosphere and worship music opens our heart and causes our spirit to rise in adoration. Worship is the love call of the saints and as we simply love and adore Him, we will experience the richness of His presence in even greater degrees.

Soaking does quieten the flesh and allows our spirit to ascend. As this happens, we become conscious that we are a spirit that lives inside a body. As our spirit starts to rise up in adoration and communion with the Lord, we can get to the place where our body is totally at rest, but our spirit is awake and receiving from the Lord (Dan.10:9).

The Results Of Being In His Presence

Revelation is often the fruit of soaking in God's presence.

The scope of all that is made available to us, as we soak or wait upon the Lord, is revealed in Psalm 27. David climaxes this psalm with his declaration in verse 14.

Ps. 27: 14 "Wait on the Lord; be of good courage, and He shall strengthen your heart; wait, I say, on the Lord!"

The exhortation to wait on the Lord is the key to everything that David expresses within this psalm.
v. 1 – 3 confidence and strength in facing the enemy
v. 4 – 5 his desire to dwell in the house or presence of God all the days of His life
v. 6 – 8 sacrifices of joy and the seeking of God's face
v. 9 – 13 victory over the enemy and seeing the goodness of God

All these things flow from the presence of God and are laid hold of through waiting on God - or in other words, through soaking in His presence.

Is. 30: 15-17 "For thus says the Lord God, the Holy One of Israel: "In returning and rest you shall be saved; in quietness and confidence shall be your strength." But you would not, and you said, "No, for we will flee on horses" - Therefore you shall flee! And, "We will ride on swift horses"- Therefore those who pursue you shall be swift! One thousand shall flee at the threat of one, at the threat of five you shall flee, till you are left as a pole on top of a mountain and as a banner on a hill."

The Lord encourages us here that salvation, which means wholeness, stems out of returning and resting in Him. This is a picture of soaking, and speaks of trusting in what He alone can do. The fruit of resting in Him is quietness and confidence. This becomes the source of our strength.

Unfortunately our flesh is very strong and wants to rule. Our tendency is to want to do, do, do. Soaking in God's presence is an insult to the flesh because it is required to do nothing. This is what these people struggled with, and they refused to return and rest in God. As a result they discovered that their fleshly abilities were not equal to the assignment against them. They thought that their "horses" were strong enough to get them through and when their efforts failed, they did not turn to the Lord, but doubled their efforts. The result was that they were left as a pole on top of a mountain. Literally, it means that they were a tree stripped of its branches. In other words, they had no fruit and appeared lifeless.

Verse 18 "Therefore the Lord will wait, that He may be gracious to you; and therefore He will be exalted, that He may have mercy on you. For the Lord is a God of justice; blessed are all those who wait for Him."

How gracious the Lord is! Because they would not wait, He waited until they were as a lifeless pole and He was exalted. Then He could minister to them. How much better it is for us to wait on Him! Someone has to wait. When we choose to be the one that waits, then the Lord is able to be gracious, have mercy, reveal His justice and bless our lives. What wonderful fruit, and all because we chose to wait on Him.

Soaking is worth the effort. It takes time and it takes dying to self but the rewards are great. Not only do we increase our awareness of the Lord's presence, but all the fruit or benefits of His presence are released into our lives.

Soaking is something that can be done privately in our own home whenever we choose. There is something powerful however about doing it in a group. When believers gather together there is a corporate anointing and finding the presence of God is easier.

Enter in, and enjoy!

(Pam Watson, Secret Place Ministries)

NO 3. INTERCESSORY PRAYER

Genesis 18; Exodus - Moses; Ezekiel 22:30; 2Corinthians 5

To intercede means to act as a go-between. To mediate between two (opposing) parties. As we execute our priestly ministry The SPIRIT will lay a more specific and greater burden for a particular individual or situation. Yield as HE does this.

____

____

LESSON 4

PRAYING IN TONGUES & "IN THE SPIRIT"

THE BAPTISM OF THE HOLY SPIRIT (Part 1 of 3)

Scripture: *Acts 2:4; 10:46; 19:6; 8:15-18; 9:17;*

This is one of three sections where we'll look at the various gifts that come from The HOLY SPIRIT as HE fills us. These gifts can be divided into three classes: -

1. **PRAYER GIFTS –** *Praying in The Spirit, Tongues, Interpretation of Tongues*

2. **PROPHETIC GIFTS** *–Prophecy, Word of Knowledge, Word of Wisdom, Discerning of Spirits*

3. **"APOSTOLIC" GIFTS –** *Gifts of healing, Faith & Working of Miracles*

Here we'll look at what for the most part is the first sign of being filled with The SPIRIT – *praying in tongues*, and then we'll go a little deeper and look into bringing a message from GOD as we *speak a tongue* and finally receiving grace to *interpret a tongue.*

Three times in the book of Acts we find people speaking in tongues after being baptized in The SPIRIT. On two other occasions it is not clear what was the manifestation that they had received but something was clearly visible. On one other occasion they also prophesied.

The baptism of the HOLY SPIRIT opens up the ability to receive and operate in all the gifts of The SPIRIT. This baptism is the first step. The first sign that we have received is speaking in tongues as a personal prayer language for our edification. Note that this is the primary use for tongues – personal upbuilding.

NOTE: It's not (primarily) so we can speak to people of different tribes. The people on the day of Pentecost were Jews from all over the world who in addition to the language they spoke in the land they were pilgrims from also spoke Hebrew as they were Jews. That's how people understood Peter when he addressed them!

____

____

____

No 4. Prayer In The Spirit

1Corinthians 14:14,15; Ephesians 6:18; Jude 20

The term 'prayer in the spirit' is used three times by Paul and once by Jude. Several of the types of prayer we'll look at can be prayed both with our minds (our natural understanding) as well as in the spirit (in tongues). Some forms of prayer however can't be done apart from in tongues. When praying in tongues we could be either communicating with GOD or with other forces in the spirit realm. We could be doing either of several things: -

    i.   Speaking to GOD

    ii.   Speaking mysteries into the spirit realm

    iii.   Edifying & building ourselves up

Note that in this class of praying in tongues interpretation is optional. Why? We're speaking to GOD! Not the other way round. Most of what we are saying is a mystery.

____

____

____

No 5. Speaking & Praying In Tongues

1Corinthians 14:2, 18; 2Peter 3:16;

The several types and applications of both speaking & praying in tongues can be divided into three categories: - **Personal Prayer/Prayer in the spirit, Corporate Prayer** & **Messages from GOD**. Each of which has its own 'rules of engagements'; not knowing the difference will make us wrest or distort scripture.

a.   PERSONAL PRAYER

Aka praying in the spirit. This is primarily for **personal edification**. To charge your spiritman like a battery is charged, ready to go. Ready to face the day. **Praying for an**

open heaven (see below) also comes into this category. From deep inside your tongues come with great force, often with very strong emotions.

b.   **CORPORATE PRAYER.**

There are times when the whole congregation needs to pray in the spirit all at the same time. A good example is when **SINGING IN THE SPIRIT** collectively in worship. Also when there is a need to press in to the callings of GOD collectively when we're all praying the same thing as we together press in. **Praying in warfare mode** (see below) when we sense that there is a 'block' or 'hindrance' to the anointing of GOD in the spirit realm is also another good time when everyone prays together.

c.   **MESSAGES FROM GOD** *1Corinthians 14:5-13, 27-28*

This is when tongues is used as an alternative to the gift of prophecy. ***Here the direction of communication is reversed*** – it is not us talking to GOD but HIM to us. For The Body to be blessed by this there obviously needs to be someone else there graced with the gift of interpretation of tongues. (see below) There could be several correct & edifying interpretations as they are not translations.

<u>Note</u>: In the spirit we are also able to pray in several modes – petition, supplication, intercession etc

____

____

____

No 6.Warfare; Praying for an "Open Heaven"

John 1:51; Isaiah; Ephesians 6; Daniel 10;13

We learn about warfare in the realm of the spirit in these passages. In the account in Daniel the warfare needed to be fought in the 2nd heaven.

1st heaven refers to the atmospheric heaven

2nd referring to where the contention with powers etc is waged

The 3rd being where Paul was caught up to – this is where GOD dwells. *(2Corinth 12:4)*

Evil is entrenched in the spiritual realm by sin committed on the earth. From deep inside, The SPIRIT of GOD empowers your spirit and this loud and aggressive form of tongues are released to dislodge forces that are gathered against you and your personal victory.

____

____

The Interpretation of Tongues

How to tune in with your sprit to hear what The SPIRIT is saying to The Body.

How the gifts operate: The HOLY SPIRIT comes upon you and empowers you for that moment or period of time to do things you can't do naturally.

How do we receive these gifts? By desire, by pressing in – they are both __TAUGHT__ and __CAUGHT__!

____

____

____

____

LESSON 5

THANKSGIVING, PRAISE, WORSHIP & SINGING IN THE SPIRIT

38

NO 7 PRAYER OF THANKSGIVING

Psalm 100:4; Proverbs 17:22; 1Thess 5:18; 1Corinthians 10:10

If thanksgiving and praise take us into HIS Courts, then _______________ will take us out of it!!

____

____

____

NO 8 PRAYER OF PRAISE

Psalm 149; 150; Psalm 22:3; 2Chronicles 20:19-20; Acts 16:25; 1Samuel 15;
Isaiah 61:1-3; 2Samuel 6:22;

- ❖ Like a mantle PRAISE ought always to rest on us, sometimes heavier than at other times but always permeating our day and thoughts.
- ❖ Praise calls on its close cousin named "Dance" to come & join in the fun (:

<u>Thought</u>: If required to, do you have a repertoire of songs that could keep you praising all night long?

____

____

____

No 9 CLAPPING HANDS AND STAMPING FEET

Psalm 47:1

____

____

____

NO 10 PRAYER OF WORSHIP

2Chron 5:14;

In praise we sing about HIM and HIS great works, in worship we sing to whom about HIS nature.

____

____

____

NO12 PRAYER OF SINGING IN THE SPIRIT

Isaiah 6:1-3

An extremely powerful weapon and tool for bringing down The Glory & Presence of GOD Almighty – it causes HIS train to fill the temple.

42

LESSON 6

PRAYER OF REPENTANCE & FOR REVIVAL

NO 13 PRAYER FOR AN OPEN HEAVEN, (PRAYED TOWARDS GOD IN WORSHIP)

____

____

____

NO 14 PRAYER OF REPENTANCE

Psalm 51;

Evil is entrenched in the spiritual realm by sin committed on the earth. 2Chron 7:13,14 the church is called to humility and repentance to break the controlling influence of evil over a section of society.

As believers tremendous freedom and release comes when we walk in cleansing and forgiveness from our father in heaven.

When a corporate grace to pray for mercy and cleansing comes upon us we enter into what could be termed "identificational repentance" – Inotherwords we are touched and burdened by not our own sin per se but the sin of the land- the community we are a part of. So it no longer becomes us the righteous ones and them the sinners, but as Daniel and Nehemiah and Jeremiah and others prayed, forgive us LORD – <u>WE</u> have sinned.

On a personal level, we walk in victory as we learn to hold a very short account with The LORD, we walk in daily confessing of sin and cleansing from sin. Ps 51 and 1John1:6-2:2

When we walk this way, the enemy looses his footholds (strongholds) in our lives. Eph 4:6,7. When a body of believers walks in this corporately it is very effective in releasing the heart cry for revival. The spirit of pride is broken in a Christian community.

Flowing in repentance is therefore a great weapon in our arsenal of spiritual warfare tools.

Revivalists like Charles Finney say it's good to make a list of sins to be repented of and do them one by one – a thorough job.

____

____

____

NO 15 IDENTIFICATIONAL REPENTANCE - PRAYING FOR REVIVAL

Hosea 10:12; Isaiah 45:8; Psalm 144:5, 12-14; John1:23-25;

Praying in this mode requires activation by The HOLY SPIRIT almost like a spiritual gift is being activated. Having a heart of compassion helps.

Break up the fallow ground - churn things up in the realm of the spirit. By our repentance we dig trenches ready to receive the rain of the Holy Spirit. This is how the Earth must open to be ready to receive the spirit.

Picture streams of water filing up a dry river bed, after the rain the dry land is suddenly teeming with life. Salvation and Righteousness will spring up. This is how community transformation occurs.

John the Baptist came before Jesus Christ to prepare the way, his ministry was one of baptism of repentance.– he came to prepare a straight path for the Messiah. He performed no miracles yet had people flocking to him to baptize them – a very powerful ministry. There's always a need for repentance before the Lord comes.

____

____

LESSON 7

SUPPLICATION & PETITION; COMMITTAL; PRAYERS OF DEDICATION; PRAYER OF SUBMISSION & CONSECRATION

NO 16. PETITION

1Timothy 2:1; 1Corinthians 14:16,17; Judges 14; Acts 4:29-31;

This is more of a formal request, placing an issue before The LORD. After this is done sometimes the answer will come in the form of guidance from The SPIRIT on how to proceed.

NO 17. SUPPLICATION

1Samuel 1:10; Mark 7:23

Supplication carries a deeper plea to it. Entreaty

NO 18 PRAYER OF WEEPING

1Samuel

____

____

____

NO 19. PRAYER OF COMMITTAL

Acts 20:32

____

____

NO 20. PRAYERS OF DEDICATION

1Kings 8:23-53

____

____

NO 21. PRAYER OF SUBMISSION & CONSECRATION (Towards GOD)

Genesis 28;20-22; Acts 21:14

NO 22. PRAYERS OF ENQUIRY

1Samuel 30;

LESSON 8

PRAYER OF AGREEMENT, UNITY, BINDING & LOOSING, THE PRAYER OF FAITH, DECREES & PROCLAMATIONS

54

NO 23. PRAYER OF AGREEMENT, UNITY,

Genesis 11; Ecclesiastes 4:9-11; Matthew 18:19; Psalm 133; 1Peter 3:7; Ephesians 4:2

Unity leads to extraordinary power being made available to us in prayer to bind (disallow) or loose (permit) things to occur on the earth in our areas of jurisdiction. This holds true from our households to our nation.

____

____

No 24: BINDING & LOOSING

____

____

NO 25 DECREES & PROCLAMATIONS

Job 22:28; Daniel4:17,24

____

____

NO 26. THE PRAYER OF FAITH

James 5:15; Mark 11:23-24; Hebrews 11:1-6; Luke 7:1-9

____

____

NO 27. PRAYER OF REBUKE, COMMAND

James 4:7;

There are times when The SPIRIT will stir us to issue forceful commands in the spirit against works of the enemy. Could be sickness, evil plots, schemes, devices etc.

"satan, I command you to desist from every manoeuvre and seize every operation against me, my household and loved ones – I decree you will not harm them in any way in JESUS name! I bind you, I cancel all your plots, I thwart every counsel of hell against me in JESUS name! "

____

____

____

____

LESSON 9

INTERCESSION, TRAVAIL, BIRTHING & GROANING IN THE SPIRIT

28. PRAYER OF TRAVAIL, BIRTHING & GROANING IN THE SPIRIT

A birthing of souls as we pray and travail in The SPIRIT. Again it operates like a spiritual gift, we create conditions that may be amenable to The SPIRIT and wait for HIS burned and gracing to pray.

1 Samuel 1:10, 12 & 13, 17 & 18; 2 Corinthians 4: 3 & 4; 1 Timothy 6:12; 2 Timothy 2:26; 2 Corinthians 10:3 – 5; James 3:17 & 18 and 5:7 & 8; Proverbs 11:30; Daniel 12:3; Matthew 9:37 & 38 Gal 4:19, Is 66:8; 1 Kings 18: 41

Elijah prayed with his head between his knees, (this was the same position Hebrew women gave birth) he knew something was coming. He had to 'birth' the new thing and pray it through.

Isaiah 66: 7-9

As soon as the labour begins, the child is birthed instantly. There is some labour before the new thing can come into being. God says that once the labour has started he will not stop it (would not close the womb)

____

____

____

There will be a birthing! This is a confidence we have in God that he will not stop once the new thing has begun. *Galatians 4:19* – going through labour pains again – there will be a birth.

Luke 2 – There needed to be background prayer surrounding Jesus' birth to protect him from harm. Simeon – 'eagerly awaiting the Messiah'. Anna – was in tune with the spirit by praying and fasting, she was a known prophetess. They prepared the way for the infant Messiah to be birthed into this world.

I will build my church, but there are certain things you need to do to affect certain things in the spiritual realm.

Zechariah 10:1 – You need to ask for rain (even in spring when the rain is plenty!)

Daniel 9:1 – Daniel had been given the prophetic words that something would happen, yet someone still had to birth it, make it happen, pray for the will of God.

The LORD will put a burden on the hearts of people who catch the prophetic words so they will pray to discover GOD'S will. The FATHER says, "Work with me"

____

____

____

____

LESSON 10

PRAYERS FOR HEALING &
THE PRAYER OF
DELIVERANCE

62

No 29. Prayer for Healing

Exodus 15:26; 23:25,26; Isaiah 53:4-6; Psalm 103:3-5; 107:19-20; Proverbs 4:20-22, 23;

Malachi 4:2; Matthew 8:17; Acts 10:38; Romans 8:11; James 5:14-16; 1Peter2:24; 3John vs 2;

<u>Question</u>: Will your body end your sojourn or will you outlast your body? Decide. *Phil 1:23-24*

____

____

A few great characters . . .

Desperate Dan

Mk 2:4; Lk 5:17;
Intrepid Ingrid

Mk 5:27; Lk 8:46;
Shouting Tim Tim

Lk 18:39; Mk 10:48
Syro-Phonecian Greek

Mk 7:27; Matt 15:23

____

____

____

MORE SCRIPTURES AND CONFESSIONS OF FAITH.
For this reason JESUS came to destroy the works of the devil. 1John3:8

GOD anointed JESUS of Nazareth with the HOLY SPIRIT and with power, who went about doing good, healing all who were oppressed of the devil for GOD was with Him.
Acts 10:38

DECLARATION

So I destroy & cancel every work of sickness, everything contrary to good health, every illness in this body in JESUS name, satan I command you to take your sickness and disease and injury and go from me now! I speak to you my body, I command you, 'BE WELL, BE STRONG, BE MADE WHOLE, WORKING AND STRONG!'

____

____

Resist the devil and he will flee from you. James 4:7
The thief only comes to steal, kill and destroy. I am come to give life, life in all it's fullness. John 10:9,10

If the spirit of Him who raised JESUS from the dead lives in me, He who raised JESUS from the dead will also give life to my mortal body through His Spirit who lives in me. Romans 8:11

DECLARATION

So in JESUS name, 'I RESIST YOU SICKNESS, IS SAY GO FROM ME NOW IN JESUS NAME!!' I resist every attempt of sickness to come to my body. I release life, I release health, I release healing and recovery in JESUS name!

____

____

Let the weak say I am strong

Joel 3:10

The inhabitant of the land shall not say I am sick
Isaiah 33:20

Say to the righteous it shall be well with him
Isaiah 3:10

DECLARATION

I declare I am well, I am whole, I am healed, I am strong, the healing power of GOD is at work in me. No weapon formed or made against me will work, every tongue that rises against me will be silenced, my vindication is of The LORD

____

____

NO 30. THE PRAYER OF DELIVERANCE

Mark 16:15-16; Luke 10:19; Acts 19; Matthew 28:19-20

All power is given!

A prayer to be free from all the works of the devil

My FATHER in Heaven,

Thank You for sending Your Son, JESUS to die in my place on the cross. I make Him LORD and Saviour over every area of my life. So I break every covenant or promise made knowingly or unknowingly with the devil or any of his agents through witchcraft, astrological charts, tarot cards or masonry. I break every such agreement whether it was made directly by me, or by others in my family line and lineage. I cut myself free from any such ungodly inheritance. I annul and render powerless any hold that the enemy of my soul might have had over me. I declare myself free by the power of the blood of JESUS which was shed and poured out on my behalf on the cross of Calvary. I am free to serve GOD body, soul and spirit! Praise You LORD! Amen.

66

LESSON 11

PRAYING FOR REVELATION – PAULINE PRAYERS

NO 31 PAULINE PRAYERS

Romans 15:13; Ephesians 1:15-19; 3:16-18; Phil 1:9-11; Col 1:9 –11; 1Thess 3:12; 2Thess 3:5; Hebrews 13:20,21;

- Know them by heart, pray them, and press into revelation,

"Your depth determines your height"

Now may the God of hope fill you with all joy and peace in believing, that you may abound in hope by the power of the Holy Spirit. (Romans 15:13)

Therefore I also, after I heard of your faith in the Lord Jesus and your love for all the saints, 16 do not cease to give thanks for you, making mention of you in my prayers: 17 that the God of our Lord Jesus Christ, the Father of glory, may give to you the spirit of wisdom and revelation in the knowledge of Him, 18 the eyes of your understanding being enlightened; that you may know what is the hope of His calling, what are the riches of the glory of His inheritance in the saints, 19 and what is the exceeding greatness of His power toward us who believe, according to the working of His mighty power (Ephesians 1:15-19)

That He would grant you, according to the riches of His glory, to be strengthened with might through His Spirit in the inner man, 17 that Christ may dwell in your hearts through faith; that you, being rooted and grounded in love, 18 may be able to comprehend with all the saints what is the width and length and depth and height (Ephesians 3:16-18)

____

____

And this I pray, that your love may abound still more and more in knowledge and all discernment, 10 that you may approve the things that are excellent, that you may be sincere and without offense till the day of Christ, 11 being filled with the fruits of righteousness which are by Jesus Christ, to the glory and praise of God.(Phil 1:9-11)

____

____

For this reason we also, since the day we heard it, do not cease to pray for you, and to ask that you may be filled with the knowledge of His will in all wisdom and spiritual understanding; (Col 1:9)

____

____

And may the Lord make you increase and abound in love to one another and to all, just as we do to you, (1Thess 3:12)

____

____

Now may the Lord direct your hearts into the love of God and into the patience of Christ. (2Thess 3:5)

____

____

Now may the God of peace who brought up our Lord Jesus from the dead, that great Shepherd of the sheep, through the blood of the everlasting covenant, 21 make you complete in every good work to do His will, working in you what is well pleasing in His sight, through Jesus Christ, to whom be glory forever and ever. Amen.(Hebrews 13:20)

____

____

____

____

____

LESSON 12

LEADING PRAYER MEETINGS - TYPES & STYLES

MOVING FROM 'ORDINARY' PRAYER TO 'PROPHETIC' PRAYER

In prophetic prayer, we first wait on The LORD in worship to receive HIS burden and direction for the meeting, our prayers are then in response to what HE has shared or burdened us to do. This can often make the prayer time more inspired, lively & fervent as it is energised out of being more 'spirit led' and empowered. These are various forms a prayer meeting can take: -

FREE FLOW MEETINGS

In these you get into worship and flow along allowing The SPIRIT to take you wherever HE desires to.

Keys needed:

- Good worship led by someone with a good & anointed voice or from CD's.
- Sensitive leadership who will be able to discern the flow and direct the meeting in that direction while allowing contributions from people along the way.
- Mature people who will not hijack the meeting and spend all the time praying about their pet project or issue.

Qn: When and how do I say STOP to someone who is taking the meeting off-course?

Answer: Come alongside them and in love and gentleness lead them round to the direction that you are meant to be going in.

Every meeting needs leadership and biblical balance. The instruction to 'not quench The Spirit' does not absolve leaders of a responsibility to oversee and administer a prophetic flow.

FOCUSED PRAYER MEETINGS

For when it is necessary to pray from a list or passage, this could be because:-
a) There is a need to focus on a need, event, or nation etc
b) It was necessary for The HOLY SPIRIT to prepare the leader ahead of time on what and how to pray.

The leader explains the prayer point after which he releases the people to pray. This is best done with the people being encouraged and inspired to pray out loud, releasing the power of GOD through their words. After each point someone is given an opportunity to 'round up' the prayers. Whoever does so, at the end gives people an opportunity to agree with an, 'amen!'

____

____

SPLITTING INTO GROUPS

Here, after the leader has explained the focus of the prayers, people are encouraged to split up and pray in different groups of usually about four or five people each. The groups may be given different topics to cover. This gives an opportunity for each person to pray while others listen in.

SIMULTANEOUS PRAYER

Acts 4:24

This can be very exciting when there is a level of enthusiasm present that enables everyone to lift up their voices all together in unison.

This can also be done in The SPIRIT as we pray in tongues together

____

____

____

A prayer to receive JESUS as your LORD and SAVIOUR from sin and it's consequences – separation from GOD and judgement

Dear LORD JESUS,

I believe that you died on the cross for me. I believe that you died in my place for all my sins, all that I have done wrong. I thank You that You loved me enough to give Your life as a sacrifice for mine. I receive your love for me right now; I ask that you take away my sins and all that has been wrong in my life. Please wash me clean and come to live in my heart. I accept you as my LORD and Saviour. Thank you for saving me, for coming into my heart and life. I love you and receive the eternal life that You give right now. Thank You LORD JESUS! Amen.

A prayer to receive the baptism of The HOLY SPIRIT and His gifts

Dear FATHER-GOD,

I thank you for sending JESUS I have received as my LORD and Saviour. Thank You that I now qualify for Your promise to also me to be filled with the power of The HOLY SPIRIT. I come to You on the basis of Your Word, the Bible and right now ask You to fill me, drench me and flood me to overflowing with Your precious gift of the HOLY SPIRIT. HOLY SPIRIT I receive You into my life now in a unique, personal, powerful and special way. Thank You as You fill me, for the gifts You also have to give me especially the divine ability to speak in other tongues and prophecy. I ask for and believe You for these gifts to show up in my life right away! Thank You my FATHER! Thank You LORD JESUS! Thank You precious and dear HOLY SPIRIT! Amen.

Other books by the same author

1. **LEST WE FORGET** – The life and times of the pioneer missionaries to Ibadan, Nigeria (1851 – 1868) As a young girl Anna's dream was to one day be a martyr for JESUS. This is the powerful story of her life along with her husband David, who were the first Christian missionaries to Ibadan in southwest Nigeria from 1851 to 1868. As you read it you will be impacted by a life on fire for GOD!

2. **THE WELLS OF OUR FATHERS -** A history of revival in southwest Nigeria from 1830 to 1959. But this is far more than a history lesson, this is about honouring the lives of all who have gone before us and laid foundations. It is on these foundations that we stand and ascend to the next levels of faith and reformation that The HOLY SPIRIT has in store for us. Life and grace are released as we honour these generals, prophets and apostles who have preceded us. We owe them.

3. **TRANSITION** – Something new is on the horizon! Highlighting areas that The HOLY SPIRIT is revealing to His saints where emphasis and change are needed to break old moulds and be supple to be able to contain the new wine falling on the church. This book starts off with a list of 25 such areas then hones in on six of them including restoration of the prophetic and apostolic offices.

4. **CROSSOVER!** – A manual for transcending societal & cultural obstacles for maximum impact. This book is a reminder of the love The FATHER has for the cultures and nations of the world. Featuring practical ways for social contextulisation including how to conduct socially open church services and contemporary evangelistic paradigms. The FATHER's love is portrayed for us as individuals freeing us to our unique and precious identities.

5. **YOU CAN PROPHESY! 70 truths about the gift of prophecy -** A handy and concise resource covering 22 Reasons to Prophesy, 7 Ways to Prepare for Prophetic Words and Encounters, 7 Ways to Activate Prophetic Grace and loads more. This book presents prophesy as a gift available to every believer, it is not a mark of some great level or height of spirituality.

6. **TRAINING & ACTIVATION MANUALS** – *Equipping the saints (Ephesians 4:11)* - Three resources for training in all righteousness that the man of GOD may be fully equipped in primary areas of the faith. – *Equipping the saints (Ephesians 4:11)*

    a. **25 types of Prayer, Tongues and Interpretation** – all in one manual. LORD teach us to pray was the cry of the disciples, 'LORD make it ours too!'

    b. **Prophecy and Prophetic evangelism** – this gift belongs to us! It is not just for the super saint! Covering all the basics you need to walk in prophecy as your spiritual inheritance.

    c. **Faith, Working Of Miracles & Gifts Of Healings – 21 ways GOD heals today!**

CPSIA information can be obtained
at www.ICGtesting.com
Printed in the USA
LVOW02s1409040417
529575LV00024B/396/P

9 781537 035550